USA TODAY **TEEN WISE GUIDES**
A GANNETT COMPANY
TIME, MONEY, AND RELATIONSHIPS

SHOPPING

SMARTS

How to Choose Wisely, Find Bargains, Spot Swindles, and More

ANNA SCHEFF

TWENTY-FIRST CENTURY BOOKS / MINNEAPOLIS

Twenty-First Century Books
A division of Lerner Publishing Group, Inc.
241 First Avenue North
Minneapolis, MN 55401 U.S.A.

Website address: www.lernerbooks.com

Library of Congress Cataloging-in-Publication Data

Scheff, Anna.
    Shopping smarts : how to choose wisely, find bargains, spot swindles, and more / by Anna Scheff.
        p.   cm. — (USA TODAY teen wise guides: time, money, and relationships)
    Includes bibliographical references and index.
    ISBN 978-0-7613-7017-8 (lib. bdg. : alk. paper)
    1. Consumers' preferences—Juvenile literature. 2. Consumer education—Juvenile literature. 3. Consumer protection—Juvenile literature. I. Title.
HF5415.32.S324 2012
381.3'3—dc23   2011021547

The images in this book are used with the permission of: © Tony Avelar/Bloomberg/Getty Images, p. 4; © Peter Cade/The Image Bank/Getty Images, pp. 5, 10; © Tony Hopewell/Digital Vision/Getty Images, p. 6; © Redshorts/CORBIS, pp. 6—7; AP Photo/Carolyn Kaster, p. 9; AP Photo/Evan Agostini, p. 11; © Minneapolis Star Tribune/ZUMA Press, p. 12; © Susan Watts/NY Daily News Archive/Getty Images, p. 13; © David McNew/Getty Images, p. 16; © Todd Strand/Independent Picture Service, pp. 18 (top), 48; AP Photo/Craig Lassig, p. 18 (bottom); © Jack Gruber/USA TODAY, p. 20; © Marc Romanelli/Photodisc/Getty Images, pp. 20—21; © James F. Dean/Workbook Stock/Getty Images, p. 22; © Sam Dao/Alamy, p. 23; © iStockphoto.com/Ljupco, p. 27; © David J. Green-lifestyle themes/Alamy, p. 30; © Reza Estakhrian/Riser/Getty Images, p. 31; © Yellow Dog Productions/Taxi/Getty Images, p. 32; © Jupiterimages/Comstock Images/Getty Images, pp. 32—33; © Brie Cohen/Independent Picture Service, p. 33; © Lisette Le Bon/SuperStock, p. 34; © Inti St Clair/Blend Images/Getty Images, p. 35; © Oredia/Alamy, p. 36; AP Photo/Journal Time, Mark Hertzberg, p. 37; © Frbird/Dreamstime.com, p. 38; © John Lund/Marc Romanelli/Blend Images/Getty Images, p. 39; © David Young-Wolff/Photographer's Choice/Getty Images, p. 41; © P. Broze/Getty Images, p. 44; © allesalltag/Alamy, p. 46; © Jason Stitt/Dreamstime.com, pp. 46—47; © Jupiterimages/Brand X Pictures/Getty Images, p. 50; © Shawn Thew/epa/CORBIS, p. 52; © Ben Welsh/age fotostock/Getty Images, p. 54; © David Goldman/USA TODAY, p. 58.
Front cover: © Emmerich-Webb/Stone/Getty Images.

Main body text set in Conduit ITC Std 11/15
Typeface provided by International Typeface Corp

Manufactured in the United States of America
1 – PP – 12/31/11

CONTENTS

INTRODUCTION
A BIG Decision

The day is finally here. You've flipped burgers and saved birthday and holiday checks for months. You've got enough cash to buy your own smartphone, but which one should you buy? You've looked at

Earning enough money to buy the latest smartphone takes hard work, so use shopping smarts to find the phone you want at the best price.

so many providers, brands, features, and colors that your head is almost spinning. How can you make sure you get what you want—and for the best price?

Relax! The best way to make good shopping choices is to be an informed consumer. When you're done reading this book, you'll know how to make the right choices the next time you go to the mall or visit an online store.

1 THE WISE
Consumer

When you decide which brand of shoes to buy or opt to stop at your local coffee shop for a latte instead of having coffee at home, you are making a consumer choice.

What exactly is a consumer? A consumer is anyone who uses goods or services—from a baby eating the mashed carrots his parents have bought to a senior citizen buying a retirement condo. *As a teenager, you make consumer choices every day.* What will you eat for breakfast? Will you grab a bowl of cereal at home or stop at your favorite coffee shop for a latte and a bagel? Will you wear your Vans or your Nikes? Will you hop on the bus to school or borrow your mom's car? That's a lot of choices, and you haven't even made it to school yet.

Is one choice better than another? Definitely—because most of the things we consume cost money. To get the most and the best-quality goods and services for your money, you need to be a wise consumer.

DO YOU REALLY NEED IT?

The first step in making good consumer choices is separating your wants from your needs. *Everyone has basic needs.* Food, clothing, and shelter—our survival depends on them. Needs are things we truly can't do without.

Wants, on the other hand, are things we desire but that we don't necessarily need. A new sports car, the latest MP3 downloads, and a top-of-the-line smartphone are all wants. You can survive without them. Water is a need—you'll die if you don't drink water for a few days. But skipping an espresso or an energy drink won't hurt you a bit.

Some needs go beyond food, clothing, and shelter. For instance, if you have a job delivering pizzas, you'll probably need your own car. If you're a student, you might need a laptop computer. When making decisions about spending money, always take care of your needs first. If you've got money left over, then the fun begins. That's when you can start thinking about your wants.

PINPOINT YOUR NEEDS

Suppose you're shopping for a laptop computer. Do you just go out and buy the first one you see? No, you think about which computer best suits your needs. Do you need one only for e-mail, surfing the Web, and doing homework? Or are you a budding graphic artist who uses the latest photo editing software? Or are you a gamer who wants a computer with the best possible speed and graphics?

IMPULSE BUYING

You're standing in the checkout lane, and a rack of candy bars is staring you straight in the face. You grab one, pay for your purchases, and start munching the moment you hit the parking lot. Congrats—the store loves you. That's because stores count on customers buying on impulse. An impulse is a sudden urge or a quick decision.

Impulse shopping is the reason stores display candy; gum; magazines; and other small, low-cost items in checkout lines. The stores want you to buy the items without putting much thought into it. Stores earn lots of money—and consumers end up spending a lot more than they planned—because of impulse buying. Impulse buying can happen online too. It can be easy to keep clicking the mouse and filling your virtual shopping basket with items you hadn't planned on buying.

It can be hard to avoid impulse buying. But you can kick the habit by thinking carefully about your budget as you make each purchase.

Stores put rows of candy bars at the checkout lane in hopes you will buy one without giving it any thought. Stores earn lots of money off impulse buying.

Knowing exactly how you'll use a product will help you make the right decision. You won't waste money on a powerful, expensive computer with features that you don't really need or end up with a bargain-basement system that doesn't get the job done.

Don't buy the first computer you see. Instead, figure out what features you will need in a computer.

BRAND NAMES

Once you know what kind of product you need, you still have many choices. Suppose you're shopping for a pair of basketball shoes. You might be tempted to buy the most popular brand name, from a company whose advertisements you've seen all over TV and the Internet. Many well-known brands have a reputation for quality, but remember that you'll probably spend more for them. Lesser-known brands often offer the same quality for a much lower price.

TARGETING TEENS

For many businesses, teenagers are a prime market—to the tune of more than $200 billion per year! Many teenagers spend their own money from allowances and after-school jobs. Teens also influence how their parents spend money. For instance, teens might ask their parents to buy one brand of cereal and not another. For this reason, companies are eager to reach teens with their advertisements.

Ads are everywhere. You'll find them on TV and radio, in magazines and newspapers, and on the Internet. Companies often hire famous athletes and actors to appear in their ads, hoping fans will want to buy a product that a star uses or promotes. Companies also pay to have their products appear in TV shows, movies, and music videos that appeal to teens. Advertising is all about getting the name of a product into your brain and making you believe you want it.

Tennis champion Venus Williams promotes Powerade Zero. Companies use athletes like Williams to convince teenagers to buy their products.

DO YOUR RESEARCH

Let's say you've identified the kind of laptop you want and even chosen the brand and model. But is it really worth the money? What do experts think about this particular product? What about people who've already bought this item? Are they happy with the purchase?

Consumer magazines such as *Consumer Reports* and *Good Housekeeping* are good sources of information about products. These magazines put products through tests and rate each feature. Head over to your local library to look through consumer magazines or check out their websites. Many online companies, such as Amazon.com, let consumers write reviews of products they have already purchased. You can read these reviews to get the opinions of other shoppers.

Consumer Reports magazine is a good place to find information on products.

Sometimes it pays to do your research in person. At a store, a qualified salesperson might tell you about features or deals you wouldn't otherwise know about. But remember: the salesperson is there to sell you a product. He or she might tell you all about the benefits of a product but not about its flaws. Also remember that not all salespeople are experts on the products they sell.

TRY BEFORE YOU BUY

Ever come home with a pair of shoes that are two sizes too small?

Probably not. If you're like most shoppers, you try on shoes before you buy them. You usually try on clothes in a dressing room to make sure they fit and look good. When it comes to most purchases, *it pays to try before you buy.*

If you're buying a TV or a sound system, check out the item's performance at the store. You'll be able to judge which models give the clearest picture or offer the best sound. At some stores, you can even test makeup, lotion, perfume, cologne, and other personal care items. You can spray a little perfume on your wrist and then continue shopping. If you still like the smell after twenty minutes, the perfume's probably a winner.

CONSUMER POWER!

Smart shopping isn't only about scoring a good deal. If you're like most teens, you're concerned about many issues, from the environment to the economy. The choices you make as a consumer can have a big impact on the issues that matter to you.

GENERATION Y FORCES RETAILERS TO KEEP UP WITH TECHNOLOGY, NEW STUFF

By Richard Eisenberg

The next time you see a member of Generation Y, show some appreciation.

In *Gen BuY: How Tweens, Teens, and Twenty-Somethings Are Revolutionizing Retail*, Kit Yarrow and Jayne O'Donnell say today's teens, tweens and twentysomethings "were the least likely to cut back spending after the onset of the 2008 recession."

What's more, Yarrow and O'Donnell say the 84 million Generation Yers born from 1978 through 2000 are so influential they've changed shopping for all consumers. They call Gen Y "the taste-makers, influencers, and most enthusiastic buyers of today," who will become "the mature, high-income purchasers of the future."

Because of Gen Y, we have:

- More creative, technically advanced websites (50% of retailers redesigned their sites last year).
- A wide availability of online customer reviews (Gen Y writes half of them).
- A faster stream of product introductions (Gen Y gets bored fast).
- Bigger, more comfortable dressing rooms (Gen Yers like to bring in friends to review outfits).

Generalizing about any group this size is risky. And making broad declarations about this generation is especially dicey, because they pride themselves on being unique. Some Gen Yers loathe brands that others love. Some prefer thrift-store finds to name brands. But the authors have done their homework. They surveyed 2,000 Americans, conducted 11 focus groups, interviewed hundreds of Gen Yers, spoke with retail executives and spent lots of time in malls.

They found that Gen Y not only decides what they'll wear but often what their parents and grandparents will wear. The authors cite a Denver [Colorado] high school senior who persuaded her 70-year-old grandmother to get Uggs and her 93-year-old great-grandmother to shop at Chico's.

Says General Motors' sales and marketing chief Mark LaNeve, "Younger people teach us what's cool." One of the book's most intriguing findings is the "gaplet" between Gen Yers over 20 and under 20, which makes it hard for retailers to aim messages at the entire group.

Many older Gen Y members grew up without iPods or computers in their bedrooms and shopped within limits as teenagers. By contrast, most of today's teens have cellphones (what the authors call "their third hand") and high-speed Internet connections. The word "recession" isn't in their vocabulary.

"My younger sister is way more into stuff than I was," says Regina, 25, of San Francisco [California]. "She not only wants more, she's so much more particular about what she wants. I see young kids with $300 jeans and Coach bags."

What does Gen Y want? The authors say:
- Websites with free overnight or second-day shipping
- Brands that resonate with them, through hip celebrities or causes
- To be asked for their opinion
- Fun shopping experiences
- "Fast fashion"—pop-up stores and limited-edition items

What Gen Y doesn't want is heavy-handed advertising aimed at them. Although if the appeal comes in a 20%-off text message on their cellphone, they'll take a look.

—September 14, 2009

BUYING GREEN

According to the U.S. Environmental Protection Agency, the average American produces about 1,600 pounds (726 kilograms) of trash per year. Multiply that by three hundred million Americans, and you have a mountain of garbage. Recycling paper, glass, aluminum, and plastic is a great way to help keep that trash out of the landfills, but not producing the garbage in the first place is even better.

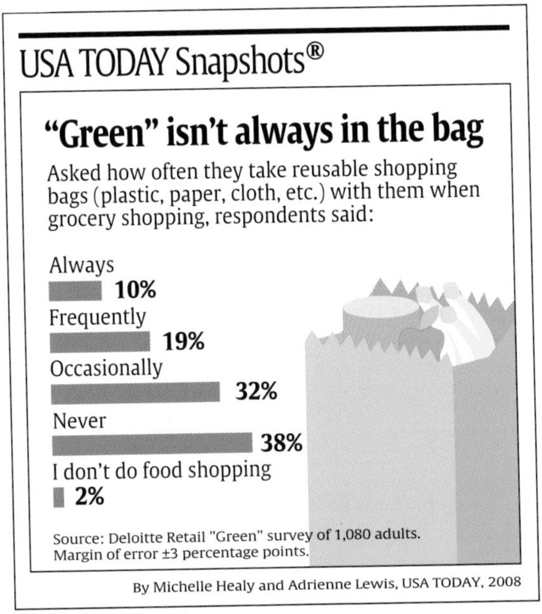

USA TODAY Snapshots®

"Green" isn't always in the bag

Asked how often they take reusable shopping bags (plastic, paper, cloth, etc.) with them when grocery shopping, respondents said:

Always
10%

Frequently
19%

Occasionally
32%

Never
38%

I don't do food shopping
2%

Source: Deloitte Retail "Green" survey of 1,080 adults. Margin of error ±3 percentage points.

By Michelle Healy and Adrienne Lewis, USA TODAY, 2008

Shoppers can help the environment just by bringing reusable bags to the grocery store. But as this graph shows, only a small portion of U.S. shoppers consistently bring bags.

Shopping with a reusable cloth bag (above) is better for the environment than taking a plastic bag.

Product packaging makes up a big part of each person's personal trash. Many products come wrapped in lots of plastic, most of which can't be recycled. Try to avoid products with excessive packaging and look for recyclable or biodegradable packaging. Biodegradable materials break down into harmless substances in the environment.

Plastic shopping bags account for lots of garbage. Instead of using them, bring your own reusable bags to the store. Instead of buying a bottle of water every day, fill up a reusable bottle with tap water. Many grocery stores sell products such as rice, beans, and flour in bulk. Bulk items don't come prepackaged in layers of plastic. Instead, you scoop or pour as much of the product as you want into a plastic or paper bag. You can reuse the bags again and again to cut down on garbage.

ANIMAL TESTING

Many teens are passionate about animal rights. Did you know that some companies test their products on animals? For instance, some health and beauty companies test makeup, soap, and shampoo on the skin and eyes of animals to see if the products cause harmful reactions, and sometimes these tests do harm the animals. If you don't like that practice, check the label before you buy a personal care product. Most companies that don't do animal testing will tell you so on the packaging. Many animal rights websites tell you which companies do animal testing and which don't. Don't buy products from companies whose practices you don't agree with.

MADE IN THE USA

Many products sold in the United States are manufactured in other countries, where wages are low. This practice might be good for a company—because it can save money on labor costs. But it also means fewer jobs for U.S. workers. To support U.S. workers, look for products labeled "Made in the USA." You'll know that the money you spend on those products will help Americans and the U.S. economy.

BOYCOTTS—POWER IN NUMBERS

If you don't like a company's products or the way it does business, you can choose to boycott, or not to buy from, that company. One person boycotting a company probably won't make much of a difference, but when

This woman chose to boycott Target in 2010 because the company donated money to a politician who opposed gay marriage.

many consumers get together for a boycott, they can often bring about change. If fewer people are buying its products, a company will start to lose money. It might change its business tactics to end the boycott.

The United Farm Workers of America (UFW) is a labor union, or a group of workers organized to fight for their rights. In the late 1960s, the UFW began one of the most famous boycotts in history. The UFW wanted to persuade grape farms in California to pay higher wages to workers who picked the grapes. The union urged consumers not to buy grapes grown in California. Many shoppers joined the boycott. It lasted more than five years and succeeded in winning higher pay for workers.

In 2010 people who supported gay rights began to boycott Target stores because the company had donated money to a politician who opposed gay marriage. Singer Lady Gaga joined the boycott. She canceled a special edition of a CD that was supposed to sell in Target stores. In response to the boycott, Target changed its donation policy in 2011.

2 SAVING *a Buck*

Before making a purchase, look for sales and compare prices from store to store.

You're getting close to buying that new smartphone, but before you shell out the money, remember that not all stores sell the same item for the same price. The price differences between stores can be huge. So do yourself a favor and comparison shop—or compare prices from store to store—before you buy.

The Internet is a great place to scout the best deals. Many stores list their prices online. Also look at advertisements in newspapers, flyers that come in the mail, and magazines. Look for coupons, sales, and other deals. *You can save big bucks by shopping around.*

FULL SALE

It may be tempting to buy back-to-school clothes in late summer and swimwear and shorts in spring, when they first appear in stores. But if you wait a bit, the item you want may soon be on sale for a fraction of the price. **Most stores discount prices and hold sales regularly.** Stores are willing to decrease prices to sell more products. Sometimes stores just need to clear the shelves to make room for new items. Other times, they're looking to boost sales or get more people in the door.

Stores regularly discount items at the end of the season. So buy your sweaters in April and your shorts in September and rake in the savings. (Make sure the clothes are roomy if you're still growing so they still fit the next season.) In late summer, expect good sales on beach gear and swimwear. Skis and snowboards are a good buy in the spring.

Some major chains operate outlet stores, which sell off-season items or overstocks—extra items that the chain wants to clear off its shelves. Outlet stores often offer good bargains, especially on well-known brands. Just remember to comparison shop, because sometimes the "deals" at an outlet store aren't any better than those you'll find at a regular store. In addition, companies sometimes manufacture items just to sell at outlet stores. These products are often of lower quality than items sold at regular stores.

Outlet stores, such as this Tommy Hilfiger outlet, sometimes offer good deals—but not always.

Some outlet stores offer items marked "second," "irregular," or "scratch and dent." These items have flaws that range from unnoticeable (uneven stitching) to major (a big scratch on a TV screen). The savings on these items can be large, but make sure you check them very carefully before buying, as they usually aren't returnable.

USA TODAY
News
SECTION A
NEWS.USATODAY.COM

CASH IN HAND, KIDS HIT THE MALL ALONE— AND RETAILERS TAKE NOTICE

By Bruce Horovitz

Something was missing when 12-year-old twins Alexandra and Elizabeth hit the mall for their back-to-school shopping: a parent.

Oh, Dad was somewhere in the mall, doing his own shopping. But his daughters, who are going into eighth grade, were each handed $150 and told to stay in touch by cellphone.

"It's about trust," says their dad, looking each of his daughters square in the eye before they set off for an afternoon of shopping. "Besides, they know what they can get away with and what they can't."

Do they ever. Off they went—regrouping with their stay-at-home dad in the mall's food court three hours later to show off their booty. And for the second year in a row, the sisters did the bulk of their back-to-school shopping on their own. "It's easier shopping this way," Alexandra says. "And less embarrassing," Elizabeth adds.

The annual midsummer trek to the mall is itself getting a makeover. A small but growing portion of the estimated $14.1 billion spent on back-to-school shopping will be made without a parent present. No, kids aren't going to the mall alone. They're going with friends. They're going with older siblings. Or they're going with groups of peers. Not just to hang out or gawk but specifically to buy school duds.

Retailers, facing a very dubious [uncertain] back-to-school shopping season, are embracing the very same kids that some once tailed around the store.

This isn't just about trust. It's about two-income couples who are strapped for time. It's about parents who believe it makes kids fiscally [financially] responsible to shop without them. It's about parents who don't want to waste limited family time at the mall.

It's about kids who feel increasingly uncomfortable with parental preferences for conservative [traditional] fashion styles and end-of-season sales. It's about kids who know that shopping with Mom typically means younger siblings must tag along, too. It's about kids who can go online and almost instantly find out what fashions have the back-to-school buzz.

And it's about parents who say they're opting to let their kids win the smaller battles—such as selecting back-to-school clothes—so that parents can focus on winning more critical battles over alcohol, drugs and sex.

"There are so many other stresses between mothers and daughters," says Nancy Taylor, an attorney and the mother of Alexandra and Elizabeth, who vividly remembers a frustrating shopping trip with her daughters some months ago that ended in tears. "Why add unnecessary ones?"

Some kids say they feel empowered by the experience of shopping without Mom or Dad.

"My mom is cool," says 13-year-old Elissa of Arizona. "But sometimes she makes me choose styles I don't like just because they're on sale." So she was happy to hit the mall—$200 in her pocket—with her best friend, Katie. The moms each dropped their daughters off, with cellphones in hand.

Not that everything went perfectly. Elissa's mom wasn't exactly thrilled with her daughter's purchase of a $27 pink seat-belt-like fashion belt and the $60 black-and-pink Vans sneakers to match. Then, there was the nearly $10 that Elissa blew on the chili dog and munchies in the food court.

"Hey, a girl's gotta eat," explains Elissa, who literally ate up one-twentieth of her shopping budget and came home with, essentially, one new outfit.

"By October, she'll be saying she needs more," says her mom. But the experiment worked, she says. "I want her to feel more like an adult, to be her own self."

—*August 11, 2003*

REWARD ME

Stores want your business. They want you to come back and buy again and again. To keep shoppers coming back, many stores use shopping rewards programs. The store keeps track of a customer's purchases, awarding points for each dollar spent. When you've built up enough points, you get a reward—often a certificate for money off your next purchase at the store. Many stores send coupons and ads for upcoming sales to their shopping rewards customers.

Should you join a shopping rewards program? That depends. If it's a store you shop at a lot, the rewards program might be worth your while. But know that the store will probably also send you lots of advertisements by mail and e-mail. If you don't want to be pestered, you might want to steer clear.

BULKING UP

Suppose you find an incredible deal on a product you really love. Maybe cases of your favorite soda are on sale for a fraction of their usual price. Time to bulk up, right? Not necessarily. Sure, you'll get a good price and won't run out for a while, but you have to consider both your budget and the amount of storage space you have. Plus, some items won't stay fresh for long. You don't want your giant carton of cookies to go stale before you've had a chance to eat them.

How do you know when buying in bulk is really saving you money? That's where unit pricing comes in handy. Unit pricing lets you compare the cost of a single unit or measurement in a package. For example, suppose a carton of twelve cans of soda costs $4. That means each can in the carton costs about 33¢ ($4 divided by 12). Suppose a carton of twenty-four cans of the same soda costs $6, so the unit cost there is 25¢ ($6 divided by 24). You'll pay more at the register for the carton of twenty-four cans, but you'll also get a lot more bang for your buck.

Many stores include the unit pricing right on the shelf tag to make comparison shopping easy. If a store doesn't list the unit price, you can figure it out yourself by dividing the total price by the unit of measure. For instance, if a 12-ounce (340-gram) box of cereal costs $1.99 and a 20-ounce (567 g) box of cereal costs $2.99, divide the prices by the ounces to find the best deal. If math isn't your thing, use a calculator, such as the one on your cell phone.

MARKUPS

Most businesses exist to make a profit. When they sell you something, they expect to make money on the deal. That means that almost everything you buy costs more than it cost the seller. The difference in price is called the markup.

Not all markups are created equal. Some markups are only 5 to 10 percent of the seller's cost, but other markups are much higher. Take a cup of coffee, for example. Say you pay $3.50 for that cup at a coffee shop. But the seller's cost for the coffee is only 50¢. That's a 600 percent markup. At a movie theater, expect to pay a markup of up to 1,300 percent on your bag of buttered popcorn. (Does it still sound good?)

Movie theaters charge a huge markup on popcorn. The price may be as much as 13 times the actual cost to make the popcorn!

Clipping coupons may sound like a bore, but it can save you big bucks. You can use coupons for everything from haircuts and clothes to music downloads and pizza.

Many stores and manufacturers offer printable coupons on their websites. Some websites are devoted entirely to online coupons. Some companies offer coupons on social networking sites.

A coupon may offer a great savings, but there's a catch. *You have to remember to use it!* Don't carefully clip a coupon and then forget to bring it with you to the store. Also remember that most coupons have expiration dates, so use them soon after you get them.

Discount codes (also called promo codes) are similar to coupons. By typing in a special code, you can get a discount on an online purchase. You can find codes by typing "discount code" or "promo code" and the name of the store into a search engine. Like coupons, discount codes must be used before their expiration dates.

But don't buy an item you don't really need or want just because you have a coupon or a discount code. Use coupons and discount codes only for items that you were

USA TODAY Snapshots®

What items are consumers most likely to use a coupon for?

Nine in 10 adults have used a discount coupon to make a purchase.

- **88%**
- Groceries **63%**
- Health/beauty items **54%**
- Clothing **46%**
- Electronics **43%**
- Gifts

Source: Harris Interactive survey for Coupon Craze of 2,022 adults, Aug. 6-10

By Michelle Healy and Veronica Salazar, USA TODAY, 2009

If you look carefully, you can find coupons for almost every kind of product or service. But most shoppers use coupons to save money on groceries.

going to buy anyway. Also, make sure you comparison shop. Even with a discount, a name-brand item might still be more expensive than a lesser-known brand.

REBATES

Rebate—it's a word that makes some shoppers sing and others groan. A rebate is money that a manufacturer or store sends to you after you buy a product. *Rebates can provide huge savings.* On high-priced items such as electronics, the savings can easily reach $100 or more.

The idea sounds great, but applying for a rebate can be a pain. You have to fill out forms, submit a sales receipt, and sometimes cut out and send in the UPC code from the product package. (That's the little box or bar with numbers and black-and-white lines.) Most rebates take six to eight weeks to process, so you also have to be patient. Many people buy products, planning to get a rebate, but then don't follow through with all the steps. They never realize the big savings.

ONLINE AUCTIONS

What if you're looking for something that isn't readily found in a store? Maybe you want an old, out-of-print book or a limited edition bobblehead of your favorite baseball player. It may be time to hit the Net. Online auction sites allow you to quickly search for new, used, and collectible items available for sale all over the world.

Shopping at online auction sites can be fun, and you might find a great bargain. At most auction sites, you place a maximum bid for the item you want. Other shoppers are bidding too. If you're the highest bidder, you get to purchase the item.

It can be fun to shop on eBay and other auction sites, but some sellers are scam artists. Check the listing carefully before you bid.

But you need to be careful. Some bidders get too enthusiastic and overspend, bidding way more than an item is worth. Other bidders fall victim to scams. They end up with poor-quality merchandise or never get their merchandise at all. Before bidding in an online auction, always read the item description and inspect any photos thoroughly. Make sure to e-mail the seller with any questions you have before you make a bid—because if you're not happy with your purchase, it can be extremely hard to get your money back. Also, make sure you understand the shipping charges. A great deal might not seem so great if the seller wants an outrageous fee for shipping.

Many auction sites require buyers to be at least eighteen years old. If you're younger, you might need to have an adult do your bidding for you.

SHOPPING SECONDHAND

These days, it's cool to be green, and what's more green than buying recycled merchandise? Thrift shops, flea markets, and yard sales can offer great bargains on secondhand goods.

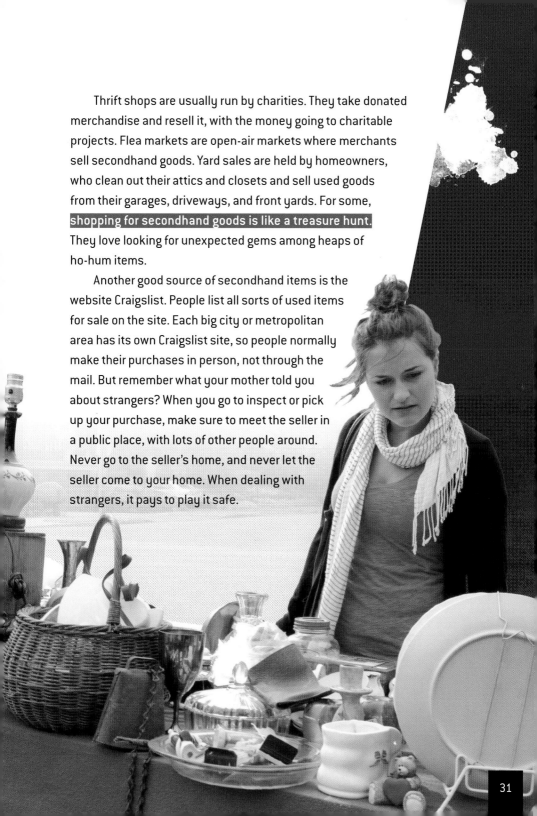

Thrift shops are usually run by charities. They take donated merchandise and resell it, with the money going to charitable projects. Flea markets are open-air markets where merchants sell secondhand goods. Yard sales are held by homeowners, who clean out their attics and closets and sell used goods from their garages, driveways, and front yards. For some, shopping for secondhand goods is like a treasure hunt. They love looking for unexpected gems among heaps of ho-hum items.

Another good source of secondhand items is the website Craigslist. People list all sorts of used items for sale on the site. Each big city or metropolitan area has its own Craigslist site, so people normally make their purchases in person, not through the mail. But remember what your mother told you about strangers? When you go to inspect or pick up your purchase, make sure to meet the seller in a public place, with lots of other people around. Never go to the seller's home, and never let the seller come to your home. When dealing with strangers, it pays to play it safe.

3 TIME TO Pay Up

Will you pay with cash, a debit card, a credit card, or a check? Each method has advantages and disadvantages.

Once you've decided what to buy and where to buy it, you're done making choices, right? Wrong! Next, you have to decide how to pay for it. As a consumer, you have a wide range of options, each with their own pros and cons.

FLASHING THE GREEN

What could be more fun than having a big wad of cash in your pocket? Even in the modern world of credit cards, debit cards, checks, and gift cards, cash still has its place. Operating on a cash-only basis can be the smartest way to keep out of financial trouble. If you don't have the cash, you don't make the purchase—it's as simple as that.

This woman writes a check. Money will be transferred from her bank account to the person to whom the check is written.

But for all its benefits, cash has its downsides. It can be easily lost or stolen. Plus, many businesses, including online sellers, don't accept cash payments.

CHECK, PLEASE

For many consumers, checks are a good alternative to cash. Checks are pieces of paper that let you transfer money from your bank account to someone else— like a friend, a store, or a charity. To use checks, you'll need to open a checking account at a bank. You'll deposit your money with the bank, and when you want to buy something, you write a check to pay for it. The payee— the person or organization that receives the check—can deposit the check into another bank account or simply trade it for cash at a bank.

GIFT CARDS

If you're like most teenagers, you like getting gift cards as presents. These cards work like cash—but only at the store that issued the card. Stores love it when people buy gift cards, for two reasons. First, many people who receive the cards forget about them and don't use them. The store gets to keep the money and never hand over any merchandise. Second, people who make purchases with gift cards often spend more than the card's value. You might go to an electronics store intending to spend your $25 gift card and end up buying $35 worth of equipment—with $10 of your own money contributed. That's great for the store, but you just spent $10 you didn't necessarily have in your budget.

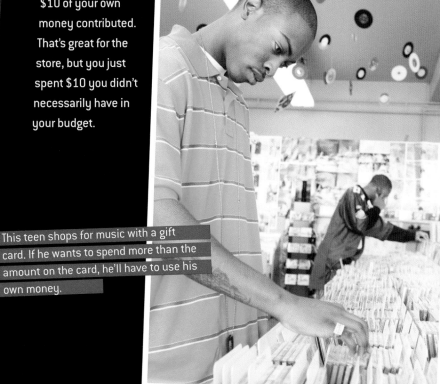

This teen shops for music with a gift card. If he wants to spend more than the amount on the card, he'll have to use his own money.

WHAT'S YOUR PIN?

To use a debit card or an automated teller machine (ATM) card, you'll need to enter a four-digit personal identification number (PIN) at the checkout counter or the ATM. This is a secret code that prevents someone else from accessing your bank account. When choosing a PIN, don't pick any easy-to-guess numbers, such as the digits in your phone number or the numbers that stand for your birthday. Don't write down the PIN and keep the numbers with your card. Instead, memorize the PIN and don't ever share it with anyone. And when you punch in your PIN at a checkout counter or ATM, make sure no one is standing too close, trying to see your numbers.

When using the ATM, make sure nobody is standing close to you when you punch in your PIN.

If you are eighteen or older, you can open a checking account at a bank. If you are younger, you'll need a parent or a guardian to help you open an account.

Checks are safer than cash because they are printed with your name, which means that only you can use them. When you write a check, you must also sign your name and sometimes show identification to the payee. The payee must also sign the check and show identification to deposit the check or trade it for cash.

At most banks, you need to be eighteen to open a checking account, but younger customers can open a joint account with a parent or a guardian. But before you and a parent open a checking account, do some research to see which bank offers the best deal. Some banks offer free checking accounts. Others charge fees for writing checks. Most banks offer an ATM card to customers. You can use the card to get cash from your account and do other banking at an ATM. But if you get an ATM card, be sure you understand any fees that go along with it.

Also be aware that if you write a check for more money than you have in your account, your bank will charge you an overdraft fee—usually around $35. To avoid overdraft fees, you must keep track of the money in your account at all times.

SALE SHOPPING ONLINE

Identity theft is a huge problem these days. It happens when someone uses your personal information (such as your name, birth date, Social Security number, PIN, passwords, bank account number, or credit card number) to gain access to your money or to buy things with your credit card. Many identity thieves find their information online, so protect yourself. Never shop online at a public computer, such as one at a library or your school. Also, shop only at websites operating on secure servers. A website with a secure server has "https" in its URL rather than "http." And remember to choose passwords that can't be easily guessed at and then keep them secret.

USA TODAY Snapshots®

Online purchasing concerns

What makes you hesitate to complete a transaction online? Top concerns:

Personal information getting stolen, sold or reused	60%
Credit card information getting stolen	59%
Receiving spam and/or junk e-mails	45%
Shipping cost	44%

Note: Multiple responses allowed

Source: Better Business Bureau survey of 1,000 adults 18 and older. Weighted to actual population proportion.

By Jae Yang and Sam Ward, USA TODAY, 2008

Shopping online offers convenience, a vast array of choices, and often good deals. But online shopping also has dangers. People especially worry about online thieves stealing their personal and financial information.

Carefully track every check you write, every deposit you make, and any fees your bank charges. When you open a checking account, the bank will give you a booklet called a transaction register, where you can keep your banking records. You can also keep track of your banking activity on a computer program such as Quicken. In addition, almost all banks let you check your account online—any time of the day or night. That way, you'll always be sure of how much you have to spend.

DEBIT CARDS

Many businesses, including many restaurants, no longer accept personal checks. That's because some people write bad checks. That is, they pay with a check but don't have enough money in their bank accounts to cover the amount. Often the business that accepts the bad check never gets paid.

What's the solution? Two words: debit cards.

Paying with a debit card is like paying with a check, but the money is immediately withdrawn from your checking account.

A debit card looks like a credit card, but it works differently. When a cardholder uses a debit card at a store or a restaurant, the money is automatically transferred from his or her checking account to the store's bank account electronically. If the customer doesn't have enough money in the account to cover the purchase, the electronic transaction won't go through.

Should you get a debit card? That depends on how responsible you are at managing your money. You'll still need to keep track of your purchases and your balance (the amount of money in your account). Plus, making debit card purchases is easy—almost too easy. You can be tempted to overspend with a debit card.

If you do decide to get a debit card, remember to treat it like a checking account, not a credit card. *If you don't have the money, don't swipe the card!* And keep in mind that some banks charge monthly debit card fees or fees for each debit card transaction. If your bank charges such fees, you'll have to decide whether the convenience of the card is worth the extra cost.

ALMIGHTY PLASTIC

Another option for paying at a store, a restaurant, or an online business is a credit card. In fact, some online businesses accept only credit cards—not any other form of payment. Using a credit card is a form of borrowing money. Every time you swipe the card at a store or enter your card number into an online site, you're borrowing money from the bank that issued the card. And that bank expects you to pay the money back!

Most people can't get a credit card on their own until they're at least twenty-one. To get one earlier, you need a parent or other adult to cosign the credit card application. By doing so, the adult agrees to be responsible for the charges if the teen can't pay. At age eighteen, you can get a card on your own, but only if you

This teen uses a credit card to buy a new shirt. She was too young to get a card on her own, so a parent cosigned the credit card application.

can prove that you have the income to pay off any charges you make. Nearly one-third of high school seniors have credit cards, either in their own names or cosigned by an adult.

Credit cards aren't for the irresponsible. Many teens— and adults—have gotten themselves into financial ruin by irresponsible credit card use. Don't be one of these people. Understand how credit cards work and use them wisely!

DEBIT CARD FEES ARE COMING: HOW TO AVOID THEM

By Sandra Block

Debit cards are convenient, widely accepted and safe. Unlike a credit card with a generous limit, your debit card will not lead you into temptation every time you go to the mall.

But, increasingly, consumers who want that kind of discipline will have to pay for it. Bank of America disclosed last week that it will soon charge customers $5 a month to use their debit cards for purchases. Bank of America will charge the fees for both PIN and signature debit card transactions, spokeswoman Anne Pace says.

SunTrust has also informed customers that it will start charging a $5 monthly fee for debit card purchases. Chase and Wells Fargo are testing a $3 monthly fee in some of their markets.

Banks say a new rule that took effect Oct. 1 left them with little choice. The rule capped the fee banks can charge retailers when customers use debit cards for purchases at 21 cents, down from an average of 44 cents.

How to avoid debit card fees:

Pay with cash. The new debit card fees will be imposed only if you use your debit card. Bank of America will charge the $5 fee if you use your debit card for purchases any time during the month. SunTrust's new $5 fee, which will apply to existing accounts starting in November, works the same way. Some retailers give customers discounts for using cash because cash doesn't trigger any transaction fees.

Be careful, though. Frequent withdrawals from an unfriendly ATM could cost you even more than using your debit card. The average surcharge for using an out-of-network ATM is $2.40, up from $2.33 in 2010, according to Bankrate.com's annual checking account survey. That's on top of your own bank's surcharge, which averaged $1.40 in 2011, according to Bankrate.

Pay with credit. At the same time banks have been adding debit card fees, they've been sweetening rewards for credit card users. For example, the Chase Freedom Visa is offering a cash bonus of $200 to new card holders who make at least $500 in purchases in the first three months.

There's a reason for this largess [generosity]: The regulation that took effect Oct. 1 didn't reduce the fees retailers pay when consumers use credit cards for purchases.

A couple of caveats [cautions]: The best rewards deals are usually reserved for customers with excellent credit. And before you substitute your credit card for your debit card, make sure you have the self-control to spend only what you can afford to pay off at the end of the month. Otherwise, the interest on your unpaid balance will make a $5 monthly debit card fee look like couch change.

"If you carry a balance, even occasionally, the interest will more than offset the meager rewards you earn," says Greg McBride, senior financial analyst for Bankrate. "Reward program or no, if there is any possibility that your credit card purchase is going to morph [turn] into credit card debt, then stick with the debit card."

Switch banks. While debit card charges are on the rise, they're by no means universal. After talking with customers, Citibank decided against charging a debit card fee, says Steve Troutner, who heads retail products for Citi's retail arm. "They told us in no uncertain terms that it would be a massive source of irritation for them," he says.

Small banks and credit unions have historically offered lower fees than the big banks, and that's likely to continue. The law mandating the reduction in debit card fees exempted banks and credit unions with assets of less than $10 billion. Many credit unions allow consumers to open an account for as little as $5.

But before you switch to a new financial institution, make sure you scrutinize all of its fees, not just those for using a debit card. For example, while Citi doesn't charge a debit card fee, it charges a $10 monthly fee for checking accounts with balances below $1,500. Citi will waive the fee for customers who arrange for one direct deposit and one online bill payment a month.

If you decide to leave your bank, you'll probably need to keep your old account open for a while to cover outstanding checks or debits. Consumers Union offers a checklist at DefendYourDollars.org for consumers who want to change accounts.

—*October 4, 2011*

Here's the scoop: When you have a credit card, you'll get a monthly statement from the bank that issued the card. The statement will list all the purchases you've made with your card that month, the total amount owed, and something called a minimum payment. Suppose you ran up $120 in charges for a month. The bank may ask for a minimum payment of $20. You pay the $20 and still owe the bank $100. But you'll also have to pay interest on that $100. Interest is a fee that borrowers pay for the privilege of borrowing money. Credit card interest can be very high—up to 30 percent. *Interest can add up fast* Say you buy a notebook computer using a credit card. The computer

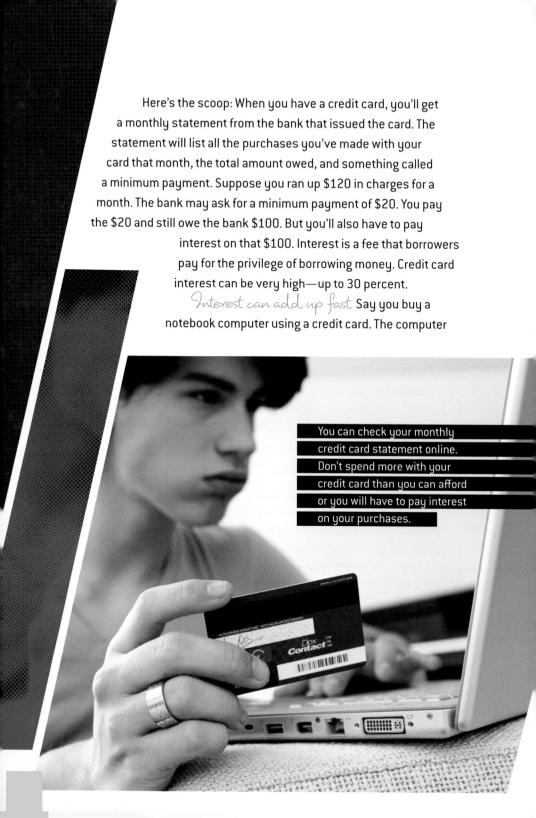

You can check your monthly credit card statement online. Don't spend more with your credit card than you can afford or you will have to pay interest on your purchases.

costs $500, and your card requires a minimum payment of $25 each month. That sounds easy enough to handle. But wait. At that rate, it will take you two years to pay off the computer. And if your interest rate on the card is 21 percent, you'll end up paying more than $100 in interest charges—and that's only if you don't use the card to buy anything else during that entire time. *Ouch!*

This may all sound like bad news, but if you're smart, you can use a credit card without paying an extra cent! If you pay off your full balance, on time, every month, you'll never have to pay interest.

SHOP AROUND

If you know you won't be able to pay off the balance each and every month, shop around for the lowest interest rate you can find. Beware of introductory interest rates. Some banks advertise very low rates, but only for the first few months or the first year you have the card. After the introductory rate ends, the interest soars. Don't be fooled! Make sure you understand the terms before you apply for a credit card. Also be aware that some banks charge an annual fee to cardholders. Look around for a card that doesn't charge an annual fee.

Many people don't know that your credit card habits can come back to haunt you later. If you're late with your credit card payments or don't make the payments at all, you'll damage your credit history. If you have a bad credit history, you might not be able to get a bank loan when you go to buy a car or a home in the future. Or you might get the loan but will have to pay an extremely high interest rate because of your poor credit history. Bottom line: don't get a credit card until you're sure you can use it responsibly and pay it off completely—or almost completely—every month.

4 I WANT MY Money Back

Always hang onto your receipts after a purchase, in case you need to return the item to the store.

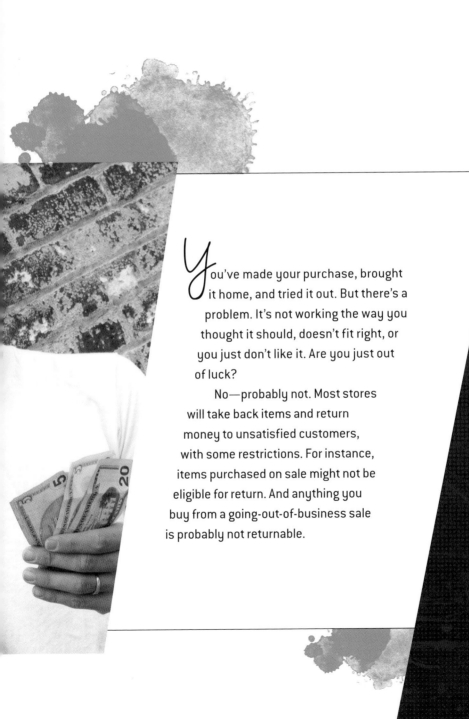

*Y*ou've made your purchase, brought it home, and tried it out. But there's a problem. It's not working the way you thought it should, doesn't fit right, or you just don't like it. Are you just out of luck?

No—probably not. Most stores will take back items and return money to unsatisfied customers, with some restrictions. For instance, items purchased on sale might not be eligible for return. And anything you buy from a going-out-of-business sale is probably not returnable.

Receipts—nobody likes them. They clutter your purse or your wallet, they get crunched in your pocket, and they slip behind the desk, only to be found months later. But receipts don't exist just to be a nuisance. They're an important part of holding onto your rights as a consumer. Many stores won't refund your money without a receipt. Other stores will give you only store credit—the chance to buy something else in the store for the same price—instead of giving your money back.

In addition to showing your receipt, you'll need to make your return in a timely fashion. Most stores have a time limit on returns—often sixty or ninety days. Some stores will take back items even after this deadline, but they don't have to, so it's better to make your return on time. After all, sixty days should be long enough for you to know whether the item is a keeper.

It's a good idea to know a store's return policy before you make your purchase. Most major chain stores list their return policies on their websites. At a local store, ask the salesperson, the manager, or the cashier about the return policy.

SWEETHEART BOOTCUT   29.50 N
827550 1402   1 @ 29.50
Trans. Discount   0.00
521 - SuperCASH Activate $10

                            29.50
Subtotal   29.50
Total   29.50
    Visa (S)
    Account: XXXXXXXXXXXXXXXX
    Auth: AUTH 459683 (A)
                            29.50
Total Tender   0.00
Change Due

Unwashed, unworn merchandise may be returned within 90 days of purchase in the country of purchase for a refund in the original form of payment for the price paid or you may apply price paid towards a merchandise exchange. A mail check will be issued within 10 days when merchandise over $5 is paid for by check or e-check. Other terms and conditions apply. Please see complete details in any Old Navy store or online at oldnavy.c

Love to shop here? Love to work her Join our team this holiday seaso Go to www.gapinc.com/jobsearch to Customer Copy

Also remember that when it comes to returns, **not all items are created equal.** If you've opened a DVD, CD, video game, or computer software, the store might not take it back. If you've worn and washed clothing, you often can't return it. Even if you've just clipped the tags off, you may be out of luck. So it's best to leave the tags on until you're absolutely sure you want the purchase—or at the very least, hang on to them.

Some stores charge a restocking fee—from 10 to 25 percent of the purchase price—to take back computers and other electronics. Stores charge this fee to cover their costs of repackaging and reformatting the product (in the case of a computer) so it can be sold again. So if your return comes with a restocking fee, you'll get some but not all of your money back.

ONLINE AND MAIL-ORDER RETURNS

When you buy online or from a mail-order catalog, you can look at pictures, but you can't examine the product in person. So be sure to check out the store's return policy before you place your order. When the item arrives at your door, you might realize that it's not exactly what you wanted.

When you buy online or by mail, a shipping company or the U.S. Postal Service will deliver your purchase. Usually, you'll pay the delivery costs. If you decide to send an item back, you usually have to pay for that delivery as well. That can end up being a very costly return!

Some online retailers offer free shipping for both orders and returns. Some stores allow you to order online but make returns in person to a local branch of the same store. To save on shipping, look for stores that offer these options.

RETURNING GIFTS

Odds are that at some point in your life, you've received a gift that just wasn't right for you. Maybe it was a duplicate of something you already had. Or maybe that plaid turtleneck from grandma just isn't your style. You probably smiled and held up the gift and thanked the gift giver. After all, it's the thought that counts, right? But then what?

If the gift giver was thinking ahead, he or she might have asked the store for a gift receipt. This kind of receipt doesn't show the price of the item, but it allows you to return a gift for a refund or store credit. If you don't have a gift receipt, you may be out of luck. You can try taking the item back to the store, but there's no guarantee you'll get a refund.

Gift cards are almost never returnable. If you get a gift card that you are sure you will never use—from Plaid Turtlenecks "R" Us, for

Everyone loves to receive gifts—but sometimes a gift is a bad fit. If so, a gift receipt can help the recipient make an exchange.

example—consider giving it to someone else or donating it to a charity. You can also sell or trade your unwanted cards on online auction sites and on websites devoted just to gift cards. You may not get the full value of the gift card if you sell it, but getting some cash is better than being stuck with a card you don't want.

WARRANTIES

A warranty is a promise made by a manufacturer or a seller to stand behind a product—that is, to guarantee it. All new products are covered by an implied warranty. That means the manufacturer or seller promises that the product will do what it is manufactured to do—as long as you use it correctly.

Most warranties don't cover deliberate misuse of the product. For instance, if you go all *MythBusters* by tossing your TV from a balcony to see if it will bounce or try to melt down gold jewelry in your microwave oven, you've violated the terms of your warranty.

When you make a major purchase, such as a TV or a car, you'll get a written warranty. This document promises that if the item stops working within a certain amount of time, the manufacturer or the seller will repair or replace it. When you make the purchase, the seller should provide you with a copy of the warranty ahead of time. The document will tell you how long the warranty lasts, how to get service if the product doesn't work, who will pay the shipping costs if the product has to be returned or repaired, what the warranty does and doesn't cover, and other limitations.

Warranties often include an owner's registration card. You can fill out the card and send it back to the manufacturer, but you don't have to. These cards are mainly a way for companies to gather data about the people buying their products. Your warranty is in place regardless of whether you send in the registration card or not.

If you watch the evening news, you've probably heard about product recalls. A company issues a recall if one of its products proves to be unsafe or defective. Recalls can apply to anything from cars to toys to food. For example, sometimes food processors recall contaminated meats or automakers recall cars with defective brakes. Companies tell consumers to stop using the product and to return it for a full refund or for repair at the company's expense.

These toys were recalled because they contain lead, a dangerous material.

How do you find out if a product you own has been recalled? If you've registered your product with the company, the company should mail you an announcement of the recall and instructions on what to do. In addition, the company will inform the media, so information about the recall will appear in newspapers and on TV and radio news broadcasts.

You can check recall information for many types of products at a government recalls website, http://www.recalls.gov. This site also allows you to file complaints about products if you feel they are unsafe.

COMPLAINTS

What if you aren't able to return an item that you're not satisfied with? What if you receive poor service at a store or a restaurant? You don't have to just put up with it. Make a complaint—but do so in a way that will make the business take you seriously.

First, call or visit the business as soon as possible after the sale or the incident and ask to speak with the manager. Going in person is your best bet, since it's easier for employees to disregard a phone call than an actual dissatisfied customer standing in their place of business. Be calm and polite as you state your complaint, keeping your voice at a normal level. If the manager isn't available, ask when he or she will be in. Leave your name and phone number, and ask that the manager call you within twenty-four hours. If this doesn't happen, make another visit to the business. Some businesses might hope you'll just forget about the complaint and go away, so you might have to be persistent.

When speaking to the manager, politely state your complaint. Provide as many concrete details as possible. For example,

USA TODAY Snapshots®

Who gets the most complaints

Industries that the Better Business Bureau got the most complaints about in 2009:

Cellphone providers	37,477
Cable/satellite TV	32,616
Banks	29,920
New-car auto dealers	26,888
Internet retail	21,494

Source: Better Business Bureau

By Anne R. Carey and Dave Merrill, USA TODAY, 2010

Customers can register their complaints about companies with the Better Business Bureau (BBB). As this graph shows, in 2009 more people complained to the BBB about cell phone providers than about other type of business.

If you have a complaint about a pair of shoes you bought, bring them to the store manager and politely explain the problem.

instead of saying, "My server was rude," give details such as, "Our table waited half an hour before the server came to take our order." If you're complaining about an item you bought, bring the item with you and show the manager the problem. Basically, the more concrete information you bring with you, the more likely that you'll be taken seriously.

If speaking to the manager doesn't resolve your complaint, you still have options. If you're dealing with a chain business, you can contact its national headquarters. Most businesses list e-mail addresses and toll-free phone numbers on their websites. You can also write a formal letter of complaint to the company's customer service department. Enclose copies of any related paperwork, such as receipts. You could even send a copy of the letter to the company's president or chief executive officer. This person's name is often listed on the company website too.

FURTHER ACTION

What if you've gone through all these steps and your complaint still isn't resolved? One option is to file a complaint with your state's Better Business Bureau (http://www.bbb.org/us/Consumer-Complaints). A consumer protection organization, the Better Business Bureau doesn't get involved with individual complaints, but it will send a copy of your complaint to the business and also list the complaint in its records. Sometimes this kind of bad publicity may be all a business needs to settle your complaint.

If the complaint is one that might involve many other consumers—as in cases of deceptive advertising or financial scams—you can file a complaint with the attorney general's office in your state, as well as the Federal Trade Commission (https://www.ftccomplaintassistant.gov). These government offices will investigate your complaint and decide whether to take legal action against the company.

IF ALL ELSE FAILS

If you exhaust all possibilities to settle your complaint, remember that you still have a powerful weapon—*your story.* Negative word of mouth can be very damaging to a business's reputation and future sales. Many websites, such as Yelp.com and BooRah.com, invite consumers to write about their experiences with businesses—both good and bad. Writing about your bad experience might save someone else from the same type of trouble.

Yelp and BooRah aren't just for complaints, however. If you receive excellent service at a business, post that as well. Excellent service is something all businesses strive for, *so if you find it, share the love!*

"YELPERS" REVIEW LOCAL BUSINESSES; WEBSITE LETS CUSTOMERS HAVE THEIR SAY ABOUT SERVICE

By Jefferson Graham

San Francisco [CA] home mover Pat Ryan says he's picked up 200 jobs since a satisfied client first raved about his moving services on Yelp, an up-and-coming website where ordinary people write reviews about local businesses.

As more customers started leaving comments, it changed the way he does business. "The reviews keep us on our toes," Ryan says. "Word of mouth is the lifeblood for a moving company."

Yelp is bringing the concept of user-generated reviews, long popular in travel and electronics, to local businesses. "Yelpers" who register at the site weigh in on everything from nail salons to car washes.

Yelpers have written more than 1 million reviews since the site launched in 2004, with more than 500,000 posted in the past four months. "If you look at the reviews on Yahoo, Google or CitySearch, they get three or four posted per business, but Yelp gets like 20 to 50," [market analyst Greg] Sterling says.

Before launching, Yelp CEO Jeremy Stoppelman was working at a business incubator brainstorming ideas for the next great website, when he happened to go online to find recommendations for a good local doctor. He came up empty. Out of frustration, Yelp was born.

"I wanted to find a way to capture recommendations online, and that made me think word of mouth," says Stoppelman, 28.

Yelp began as an e-mail recommendation service. Now, it has specific sites for nine major cities, including Los Angeles, New York, Austin and Seattle. It also has Yellow Pages information for local businesses nationally.

A search for restaurants in Kill Devil Hills, North Carolina, turned up a list of eateries along North Carolina's Outer Banks, most with one or two reviews. A search for Ted Drewes Frozen Custard of St. Louis [MO] produced a listing, photos and seven reviews.

Anyone can view listings on Yelp, but folks are encouraged to register and post pictures, write reviews and invite friends.

"We don't want people to come by with drive-by reviews, venting to get back at an establishment," says Stoppelman. "We're a community that talks to one another."

But online write-ups can be a double-edged sword, says Steve Kravac, owner of Tiny's K.O., a Los Angeles [CA] bar with 74 Yelper reviews. "You'll get positive responses from people, but there will also be people who want to harangue [hassle] you for no reason," he says.

Nathaniel Uy, managing partner of Mondo Gelato, a San Diego [CA] ice creamery, is so obsessive about reviews that when he received a 4-star rating (out of 5) from a customer, he wrote to her.

"I asked if there was anything we could do to improve," he says. "She's since come back and turned into a loyal customer."

Nick Kokonas, managing partner of Chicago [IL] restaurant Alinea, says his customers are doing more than just posting reviews of his establishment, which opened 18 months ago. "From the very first day, we've had three or four people taking pictures of our food, and posting them on sites like Yelp and Flickr," he says. "We attract passionate people who love food, art and culture, and they go online and want to tell people about what they've discovered."

Yelp encourages members of the "Yelp Elite" to gather at local parties and post on the "Weekly Yelp," a blog about local happenings. There's information on the site about everything from review etiquette to why and how some reviews get taken down. What you won't find is the meaning of the name Yelp.

That got tossed into the mix during an early naming session, recalls Simmons, and instantly rejected. "It sounded like a dog being kicked," he says.

But with no better ideas, "Yelp" kept returning.

"It's short, easy to say, and has turned into a verb," he says. "It sounds like, 'The Yellow Pages needs help,' and now, we love it."

—June 13, 2007

BEING A *Savvy Consumer*

Being a savvy consumer will help you get the most for your money.

All consumers want to get the best bang for their buck, and nobody wants to get stuck with a raw deal. By understanding how retailers operate and your rights as a consumer, you can get the most out of your shopping dollars.

Then when you go to shop for that smartphone, you won't feel confused by all your options. You'll pinpoint the features you want. You'll narrow down the brands, models, and carriers. You'll know how to compare prices, both in local stores and online. And you'll know all your payment options—and the potential advantages and downsides of all of them. And if something goes wrong along the way, you'll know how to deal with it.

Some people confuse being a savvy customer with being cheap. If you use coupons, people behind you in line at the cash register might groan and grumble. But you're the one realizing the big savings, while the grumblers are paying full price.

As a consumer, you are your own best advocate. You're the best person to determine your wants and needs and how to go about meeting them. You're also the best person to look out for your own money. With all the knowledge and tools you have learned, being a savvy consumer should be easy.

Happy shopping!

GLOSSARY

AUTOMATIC TELLER MACHINE (ATM): a computerized machine where people can do basic banking, such as withdrawing and depositing money

BOYCOTT: to refuse to buy a product or do business with a company to pressure the company to change its business practices. To be successful, boycotts must involve large numbers of people.

BRAND NAME: a product or a company whose name is well known, popular, and widely advertised

CHECK: a certificate one person fills out and gives to another, authorizing the payment of money from the check writer's bank account

CONSUMER: someone who buys or uses products and services

COUPON: a certificate entitling the user to a discount on a product or a service

CREDIT CARD: a plastic card issued by a bank, a store, or other business that allows people to pay for their purchases at a later date

CREDIT HISTORY: a record of how well you've managed your credit, such as paying off loans and credit cards on time. Businesses use your credit history to determine if they will give you new loans.

DEBIT CARD: a plastic card that allows you to make purchases at stores and other businesses. When you pay with a debit card, the money electronically transfers from your bank account to the business's bank account.

GIFT CARD: a plastic card that can be used like cash at the store that issued the card. The card is set for a certain dollar amount. The user can spend the money all at once or in increments.

GIFT RECEIPT: a receipt that does not show the dollar value of a purchase. With a gift receipt, you can easily return or exchange an unwanted gift.

IDENTITY THEFT: the illegal use of someone else's personal information, such as credit card or Social Security numbers. Identity thieves steal information to make purchases or obtain credit in someone else's name.

IMPULSE BUYING: making a purchase on impulse, or without planning. Shoppers often make impulse purchases of candy and magazines in the checkout line at grocery stores.

INTEREST: money that a borrower pays to a lender for the privilege of borrowing money

MARKUP: the difference between what a seller pays for an item and the price charged to consumers

OVERDRAFT FEE: money a bank charges if you write a check for more money than you have in your account

REBATE: money that a manufacturer or a store sends to a consumer after he or she purchases a product

RECALL: a manufacturer's announcement that a product is unsafe or defective, with instructions for consumers to return that product

RECEIPT: a slip of paper showing proof of a purchase. Most receipts are printed with the name of the seller, the date of purchase, a list of the items purchased, the price of the items, and the method of payment.

RESTOCKING FEE: a fee charged by a business to take back a returned item that has been opened

RETAILER: a business that sells items directly to the final consumer

UNIT PRICING: the cost of a single unit or measurement of a product—for instance, the price per ounce. Many stores list unit prices on shelf tags. It helps consumers compare prices between different brands and package sizes.

WARRANTY: a guarantee that a product will work as it should and that the manufacturer will replace or repair the product if it is defective

SELECTED BIBLIOGRAPHY

Beroff, Art. *Bargain Hunter's Field Guide.* Panama City Beach, FL: Avebury Books, 2003.

Consumer Reports. "Calendar of Deals—What's on Sale When." ConsumerReports.org. January 2010. http://www.consumerreports.org/ cro/money/shopping/shopping-tips/sales-calendar-7-07/overview/0707_ sales_ov_1.htm#calendar (May 9, 2011).

Deering, Kathryn R., ed. *Cash and Credit Information for Teens: Tips for a Successful Financial Life.* Detroit: Omnigraphics, 2005.

Dunleavey, M. P. "How Teens Get Sucked into Credit Card Debt." MSN Money. N.d. http://articles.moneycentral.msn.com/SavingandDebt/ManageDebt/ HowTeensGetSuckedIntoCreditCardDebt.aspx (May 9, 2011).

Pilon, Mary. "How to Complain about a Company." *Wall Street Journal*, August 5, 2009. http://blogs.wsj.com/wallet/2009/08/05/how-to-complain-about-a-company (May 9, 2011).

Spencer, Kathy. *How to Shop for Free: Shopping Secrets for Smart Women Who Love to Get Something for Nothing.* Cambridge, MA: Da Capo Press, 2010.

FURTHER INFORMATION

Better Business Bureau
http://www.bbb.org
Check this site for a list of businesses that meet Better Business Bureau standards for honesty and quality, as well as lists of businesses that have had complaints lodged against them.

Blatt, Jessica. *The Teen Girls' Gotta-Have-It Guide to Money: Getting Smart about Making, Saving It, and Spending It.* New York: Watson-Guptill Publications, 2008.
This book includes tips for making, saving, investing, and spending money wisely.

Donovan, Sandy. *Budgeting Smarts: How to Set Goals, Save Money, Spend Wisely, and More.* Minneapolis: Twenty-First Century Books, 2012.
By making a budget and sticking to it, you can make the most of your money. This book tells you how to manage your income and expenses—and end up with money in the bank.

Federal Trade Commission
http://www.ftc.gov
The Federal Trade Commission is a U.S. government agency charged with protecting consumer interests. The website contains information on many topics, including credit and loans, money management, and shopping for products and services.

Foster, Jill Russo. *Cash, Credit, and Your Finances.* Bangor, ME: Booklocker.com, 2009. This book explains living within a budget, using bank accounts, and managing credit.

It's My Life—Money
http://pbskids.org/itsmylife/money/index.html
Check out this site for all sorts of smart money tips for kids.

LifeSmarts.org
http://www.lifesmarts.org
This educational program from the National Consumers League involves an online team competition designed to teach consumer skills to teens.

Lysaght, Alan, and Denis Cauvier. *The ABCs of Making Money for Teens.* New York: Wealth Solutions Press, 2005.
The authors show you how to spot rip-offs, get a job, invest wisely, and turn your hobby into a business.

Shelley, Susan. *The Complete Idiot's Guide to Money for Teens.* Indianapolis: Alpha Books, 2001.
This book lays out all the basics on earning, spending, saving, and investing money.

Tips for Teens
http://www.themint.org/teens/index.html
This site includes information and quizzes about credit cards, how to write a check, budgeting, balancing checking accounts, and more.

LERNER

SOURCE™

Expand learning beyond the printed book. Download free, complementary educational resources for this book from our website, www.lerneresource.com.

INDEX

ABOUT THE AUTHOR

Anna Scheff is an experienced children's book author who lives in Minneapolis, Minnesota.